BACKROADS TO FAR TOWNS

BACK ROADS
TO FAR TOWNS

BASHŌ'S TRAVEL JOURNAL

Translated by
CID CORMAN AND KAMAIKE SUSUMU

Illustrated by
HIDE OSHIRO

WHITE PINE PRESS • BUFFALO, NEW YORK

Publication of this book was made possible, in part, with public
funds from the New York State Council on the Arts, a State
Agency.

First Edition

Library of Congress Control Number: 2004109162

Published by
White Pine Press
P.O. Box 236
Buffalo, New York 14201
www.whitepine.org

To the memory of Cid Corman

CONTENTS

INTRODUCTION

Early one spring morning in 1689 Bashō, accompanied by his friend and disciple Sora, set forth from Edo (old Tokyo) on the long nine-month journey which was to take them through the back-lands and highlands north of the capital and then west to the Japan Sea coast and along it until they turned inland again towards Lake Biwa (near Kyoto). Approximately the first half of this journey, the most arduous part, remains recorded in the *Oku-no-hosomichi*.

Bashō in his 46th year and Sora in his 41st had lived quietly near each other for some time. The journey was one both had looked forward to and realized would be difficult and even dangerous. And, indeed, one might not return. It was to be more a pilgrimage—and in the garb of pilgrims they went—than a case of wandering scholarship: a sight not uncommon even in modern Japan, visiting from temple to temple, seeing old acquaintances, places famed in history or poetry or legend, touchstones for the life lived, the dying to come and what life continues.

By then Bashō had already earned a far-flung reputation as a *haikai* poet and master and was much awaited and sought out: he was himself invariably the occasion *for* poetry.

Most of his poetry (and it is within the tradition which he himself was shaping) evokes a context and wants one. The poems are not isolated instances of lyricism, but cries of their occasions, of someone intently passing through a world, often arrested by the momentary nature of things within an unfathomable "order."

If, at times, the poems seem slight, remember that mere profusion, words piled up "about" event, often give an illusion of importance and scale belied by the modest proportions of human destiny. Precise conjunction of language and feeling, appropriately sounded, directness and fullness in brevity, residual aptness and alertness, mark *haiku* at best (as in those of Bashō): grounded in season and particularity, no matter how allusive. "Down-to-earth and firm-grained."

Sora also kept a journal of this trip, but it remains as a strictly factual "check," while Bashō made his into (essentially) a poem (after some years) that has become a center of the Japanese mind/heart.

We, too, move out with him to and through the backwater regions of north central Honshu. His words are our provision, breath, rhythm. And they can never not be our time. The end of his journey is the end of ours. Everywhere he goes one feels a sounding made, the ground hallowed, hardwon, endeared to him, and so to us, through what others had made of it, had reached, discovered.

So many today who have lost touch have lost touch with just such grounds for being.

When tears come to Bashō it may seem that he is merely being soppy (one might say the same of Dante or of Stendhal, though both are also "tough"). A man's sentiments, however, are not disputable. But if we feel what it is to live and to be dying, each one alone, know what cherishing is and see what Bashō sees into tears, we may realize that there is a sympathy that enlarges the spirit without destroying it and obtains for man a more complete sense of relation to his world.

What Bashō doesn't say moves at least as much as what he does. One knows his silences go deeper than reasons. And when his eyes plumb words for heart—when the heart holds the island of Sado, locus of exile, at the crest of a brimming sea—and the eye lifts from that pointed violence and loneliness on the horizon to the stars flowing effortlessly up and over and back into the man making vision, who has not at once felt all language vanish into a wholeness and scope of sense that lifts one as if one weighed nothing?

Whether, when we go to him, return to him, as many of us must when we are most alone, we feel much as he does in his last entry, elated, back with old friends, or not, remains for each to find out. But the hope is that in bringing this text into English, some will open wider for it, discover the heart's, spirit's, geography refreshed—"read" (as a Nōh teacher said apropos of reading a Nōh text) as one who has traveled and climbed and come down and who knows he has still harder going ahead "reads" a map.

Meanwhile a summer's journey awaits, two men are about to depart on foot, one of them already thinks of us.

TRANSLATORS' PREFACE

More and more we live at a time when the foreign is no longer exotic, when romantic images of past ages no longer either convince or suffice. And with this changing attitude perhaps a more salutary, more perceptive, sense of what experiences the past offered and still offers can be brought to bear in such translations as the one now before you.

If the translators have often not accepted Western approximations for particular Japanese and/or Chinese terms, it is not to create undue difficulties for readers, but rather to admit an exactitude otherwise impossible. As a result, notes may be needed in greater profusion than before.

Bashō's style is a *haiku*-style: terse and to the point, while being allusive to the degree of T'ang poetry. We have tried to maintain the feel of his sometimes unusual syntax, the flow and economy of his language. The poems should help *clot* passages, so that one doesn't read too rapidly.

BACK ROADS TO FAR TOWNS

1

Moon & sun are passing figures of countless generations, and years coming or going wanderers too. Drifting life away on a boat or meeting age leading a horse by the mouth, each day is a journey and the journey itself home. Amongst those of old were many that perished upon the journey. So—when was it—I, drawn like blown cloud, couldn't stop dreaming of roaming, roving the coast up and down, back at the hut last fall by the river side, sweeping cobwebs off, a year gone and misty skies of spring returning, yearning to go over the Shirakawa Barrier, possessed by the wanderlust, at wits' end, beckoned by Dosojin, hardly able to keep my hand to any thing, mending a rip in my *momohiki*, replacing the cords in my *kasa*, shins no sooner burnt with moxa than the moon at Matsushima rose to mind and how, my former dwelling passed on to someone else on moving to Sampū's summer house,

> the grass door also
> turning and turning into
> a doll's household

(from the eight *omote*) set on a post of the hut.

(1689)

15

2

Yayoi: last seventh, slightly hazy dawn, "a waning moon, a failing light," summit of Fuji vague, crowns of blossoming cherry at Ueno and Yanaka, when would they—and would they—be seen again? Friends, gathering since nightfall, came along by boat to see us off. Landed at Senju, sense of three thousand *li* ahead swelling the heart, world so much a dream, tears at point of departure.

> departing spring
> the birds at their cries fishes'
> eyes Amida tears

the *yatate's* first words, the path taken looked not to advance at all. Those filling the way behind watched till only shadows of backs seemed seen.

(March 27)

3

This year, the second—is it—of the Genroku, far only to think how far it is to Ōu "under Go skies," to picture hair turning white, places ears had heard of eyes never seen, likelihood of returning not so bright, just did make the post town of Soka by nightfall. Thin shoulders feeling packs drag. Body enough, but burdened with a set of *kamiko* (extra protection at night), *yukata*, raincoat, ink-stick, brushes, as well as unavoidable *banamuke*, somehow hard to let go of, part of the trouble of traveling inevitably.

4

Visited the Muro-no-Yashima. My companion, Sora, said: "The deity here, Konohana Sakuya Hime, is the same as that at Fuji. She went out and set Fire to the Utsumuro to prove her innocence and out of this was Prince Hohodemi born and the place called Muro-no-Yashima. And why poetry written about it mentions smoke." Also fish known as *konoshiro* prohibited here. Story behind it common knowledge.

(March 29)

5

Thirtieth. Stayed at foot of Mt. Nikkō. Hosteler says: "They call me Hotoke Gozaemon. Honesty's a habit with me, which is why the name, so feel right to home," what he said. Impossible not to realize how Buddha appears upon this mean and muddled ground in just such guise to help shaman beggar pilgrims on, seeing our host's simple sincere manner, frank and down-to-earth. Firm-grained and unassuming, the very image of the man *jen*, worthy of all respect.

(March 30, actually April 1)

6

First of Uzuki, called on the mountain shrine. Originally this mountain known as Futarayama, but when Kūkai Daishi dedicated the shrine here, he renamed it Nikkō. Perhaps with presentiment those thousand years ago of the splendor now gracing our skies and the blessings extended to the eight directions to the four classes of citizens living in peace. But with glory so full, so empty are words.

> how inspiriting
> the green leaves young leaves of a
> sun's resplendency

(April 1)

7

Mt. Kurokami hung with mist and still snow clad.

> with the head shaven
> at Kurokami Mountain
> changing apparel
> > (Sora)

Sora formerly Kawai Sōgorō. In *bashō* shade, eave to eave, helped at wood and water chores. Delighted at the chance to share prospects of Matsushima and Kisakata, offered to take on whatever tasks the journey would call for, at dawn of the day of departure had head shaven, assumed pilgrim garb and signalled the new life by changing name to Sōgō. And so, the Mt. Kurokami poem. The words "changing apparel" weigh tellingly.

Climbed more than twenty *cho* uphill to find the waterfall. Plunges from over cavern a hundred *shaku* down to thousand-rock-studded basin below. Stooped into cavern to peer out from behind cascade known as Urami Falls.

> only for a time
> to a waterfall confined
> summer opening

> > *(April 2)*

8

      Set out for place called Kurobane in Nasu to see an acquaintance there and tried shortcut through fields. Caught sight of a village not too far off, made for it, rain starting, evening coming on. Passed night at a farmhouse and next morning tried crossing fields again. Horse pastured there. Asked the way of a fellow mowing nearby who, plain as he was, wasn't without courtesy. "Let me see," he says, "you know this here field cuts off different ways and if you don't know which is which, worse luck, easy to get lost, so better let the horse there take you far as he can and when he stops, just send him back," and he lent us the horse.

      Two tiny creatures scampered behind. And a darling called Kasane. A curious sweet name:

> and this *kasane*
> the pretty double pink's
> name naturally

Soon at the village, tied something for owner to saddle and sent horse back.

(April 3)

9

Visited a certain Jōbōji, Kandai of Kurobane. With unanticipated pleasure talked day and night, his brother Tōsui coming over faithfully morning and night, had us to his place and then, at their instance, to relatives of his, and days passed: one in strolling about the outskirts, inspecting the site of the *Inuoumono*, another in wandering around the Nasu reed-brakes to see Tamamo-no-mae's old tomb. Then praying at the Hachiman shrine. When Yoichi aimed at and struck the fan down, the prayer he uttered was: "Above all, to Shohachiman, god of my nativeland," referring to this shrine, and the grace of that response realized touches deep. At nightfall returned to Tōsui's.

Temple there called Shūgen-kōmyōji. Invited, visited *gyoyado*.

> in summer mountains
> praying to the *ashida*
> to get on with it

10

Buried in the vicinity of Unganji the spot Butchō-sho lived in mountain retreat.

> less than five-foot square
> thatched abode
>
> a pity to put up at all
> but there *is* rain

is what he wrote with pine-charcoal point on rock—how long ago was that told? To see what remains led our walking-sticks to Unganji and some kindly beckoning others to come along too, mostly younger people, got caught up in such eager chatter, reached mountain unawares. Dense a long way through the valley, pine and cedar thick massed, moss oozing, *Uzuki* sky chilly. Where the ten views ended crossed a bridge and entered by temple gate.

Then, intent on our quest, scrambled up just beyond and there it was, the hut, perched on a ledge up against a cave. Like seeing Myōzenji's "Entrance to Death" or Hōun-Hoshi's "Stone Chamber."

> even woodpeckers
> can't break into this hut
> summer trees

hastily written, the one poem, left on a post there.

(April 5)

11

Afterwards off to the Sesshōseki on horse sent by the *kandai*. Man leading it by halter asked for a *tanzaku*. Beautiful he wanted one:

> across the meadow
> horse take your lead now from the
> *hototogisu*

The Sesshōseki in mountain shadow where hot springs flow. Noxious fumes of the rock not yet abated and such a pile of dead butterflies, bees and other bugs sand underneath hard to see.

(April 19)

12

Yes, at Ashino there's still the willow of the "pacing stream" on a path amid fields. A certain Kobu, *gunshu* of the region, had often offered to show us the tree and had wondered exactly where it was and today at last in that very willow's shade.

> a paddy of rice
> planting completed leaving
> the willow alone

(April 20)

13

Anticipation each day mounting towards the Shirakawa Barrier, but mind each day calmer clearer for continuing. Of course felt like "somehow sending word to Miyako." After all, one of the Three Barriers, and others of poetic bent left word of feeling behind. "Autumnal winds" hummed in my ears, "the maple" stood imagined, but leafgreen branches haunting too. Against *unohana* white white briars, as if pushing through snow. Here, according to Kiyosuke's brush, long ago a man put on the *kanmuri* and donned courtly costume.

> *unohana* the
> hairpin for the barrier's
> festival costume
> > (Sora)

(April 21)

14

So we went over and crossed the Abukumagawa. To left, high summits of Aizu, and to right, the demesnes of Iwaki, Sōma and Miharu, divided by mountain ranges from Hitachi and Shimotsuke. Passed place called Kagenuma, but overcast sky hindered reflection.

At post town of Sukagawa visited one Tōkyū and were had to stay four or five days. First thing he did was ask: "Anything come of crossing the Shirakawa Barrier?" What with the aches of so much traveling, with body and mind exhausted, apart from being entranced simply by the scene and remembering other times, there wasn't much chance for thinking words of my own through.

> natural grace's
> beginning found in Oku's
> rice-planting singing

is all that the crossing brought, was my reply, which, emended by a *waki* and *daisan*, led to composing three sequences.

(April 22)

15

Off on the edge of town in the shade of a huge chestnut tree, a priest, completely out of things. Perhaps "in mountain depths gathering chestnuts" referred to such an existence, or so to my imagination it seemed and, given something to write on, wrote, "literally *kanji* for 'chestnut' read 'west tree,' they say alludes to the Western Paradise, and Gyōgi Bosatsu, they say, during his lifetime used it for his walking-stick and the posts of his house."

> the majority's
> invisible flowers are
> of the eaves' chestnut

16

From Tōkyū's place about five *li* to post town of Hihada, and Mt. Asaka just beyond. Off the road a ways. Mostly marshland hereabouts. *Katsumi*-gathering time near, asking people about the so-called *hana-katsumi*, but none knew. Poking about the marshes, asking everyone met, roaming in search of *katsumi katsumi*, sun grazing mountain ridge. Turned right at Nihonmatsu and looked into Kurozuka cavern and stayed over in Fukushima.

(May 1)

17

       Next day, went around asking for *Shinobu-moji-zuri* rock, reaching Shinobu village. At a hamlet just the other side of the mountain rock, half-buried in earth. Some village children tagged along and explained. In olden times they said, it used to be up on top of the mountain, but villagers tired of people passing through tearing out their green grain to try on rock bowled it over into valley so face now hidden. Might well have been so.

> the rice-seedlings plucked
> rooted by hand from of old
> Shinobuzuri

                                        May 2)

18

Took ferry at Tsukinowa, to post town of Seno-ue. Site of Satō Shōji's to be found to the left about *li* and a half away. Heard it was at Sabano in Iizuka and kept enquiring on the way, finally locating mountain called Maruyama. Here remains of his castle are. At bottom, ruins of main gate, etc., and seeing them so, eyes fill, and at old temple hard-by, family graves. Tombs of young wives of two sons most felt. The story of their hero- ism, though women, has come down, sleeve at my eyes. The Weeping Rock can't be very different. Went into temple for tea, where Yoshitsune's long- sword and Benkei's *oi* are kept as treasures.

> the chest and the sword
> in May time raise aloft as
> the paper banners

This occurred on the first of *Satsuki*.

(May 1, actually May 2)

19

Spent night at Iizuka. Bathed at hot-springs there, found lodgings but only thin mats over bare earth, ramshackle sort of place. No lamp, bedded down by shadowy light of fireplace and tried getting some rest. All night, thunder, pouring buckets, roof leaking, fleas mosquitoes in droves: no sleep. To cap it off the usual trouble cropped up, almost passed out. The short night sky at last broke, and again picked up and went on. But the night's traces dragged, mind balked. Hired horses, got to post town of Ko'ori. Future seemed further off than ever, and recurring illness nagged, but what a pilgrimage to far places calls for: willingness to let world go, its momentariness, to die on the road, human destiny, which lifted spirit a little, finding foot again here and there, crossing the Ōkido Barrier in Date.

20

After passing Abumizuri and Shiroishi Castle, entered the district of Kasashima, and sought out To-no-chujo Sanekata's grave: far to right among slopes could be seen villages of Minowa and Kasashima, where Dōsojin shrine and susuki grass of memory remain. What with May rains the road impossible and, much too tired, gazed at them from afar, Minowa and Kasashima—apt for the season,

> Kasashima's
> where now on the month of May's
> mud-ridden highway

and put up at Iwanuma.

(May 4)

21

Stirred by the pine of Takekuma. At its roots trunk breaks into two arms, probably much as in olden times, nothing lost. Immediately Nōin-Hoshi came to mind. Before his time the Lord of Mutsu had come and had the tree cut down to help provide lumber for bridge over the Natorigawa, which may account for his writing: "no sign there now of the pine." Time and time again, said to have been replaced, cut down, and now standing, the image of a thousand years in fine shape again, miraculous.

> The Takekuma
> pine please do present to him
> o so late cherry

given me on departing by one known as Kyohaku, now elicits:

> since cherry blossoms
> yearning for the two-trunked pine
> three months later now.

22

Crossing the Natorigawa entered Sendai. Day of plaiting eaves with blue flags. Found an inn and stayed four or five days. Painter here called Kaemon. Had heard of him as one of not a little spirit and met. For many years he'd hunted up places once famous in the area but now obscure and one day showed us around. *Hagi* so thick in Miyagi Fields, could sense what fall must be like. Tamada, Yokono, and at Tsutsuji-ga-oka *asebi* flowers near peak bloom. Went through pine woods so dense sun can't penetrate, place called Konoshita. Once long ago the heavy dewfall led to, "Attendants, an umbrella" being written here. Visited the Yakushidō and Tenjin Shrine and some other places as sun descended. And he showed and gave us sketches of parts of Matsushima and Shiogama. And added two pairs of straw sandals, cords dyed dark-blue, as *hanamuke*. So, indeed, was he seen as one of true *furyu*

> ah to have blue flags
> on one's feet in the form of
> the straw sandal cords

(May 7)

31

23

       Consulted sketches as we went, skirting mountains; alongside winding Oku-no-hosomichi Tofu sedge. People here still make annual tribute of ten-stitch sedge mats to the *kokushu*.

The Tsubo-no-ishibumi found at Taga Castle in village of Ichikawa. More than six *shaku* high and maybe three *shaku* wide. Words vaguely made out through moss. Distances in *li* to the frontier at all four cross-points marked. Castle originally erected in first year of Jinki by Ōno-no-ason Azumabito, *azechi* and *chinjufu shogun*. In sixth year of Tempyō-hōji, Emi-no-ason Asakari, *sangi* and *setudoshi* for Tokai and Tozan, had it repaired. On first day of the twelfth moon, it records. Time of Emperor Shōmu. Many old places brought down to us through poetry, but landslides and floods have altered paths and covered markers with earth, and trees arisen generations gone, and hard to locate anything now, but that moment seeing the thousand-year-old monument brought back sense of time past. One blessing of such a pilgrimage, one joy of having come through, aches of the Journey forgotten, shaken, into eyes.

(May 8)

24

Then visited the Tamagawa at Noda and the Okino-ishi. On Sue-no-Matsuyama temple known as Masshōzan. Everywhere between pines graves, bringing home the fact that even vows of "wing and wing, branch and branch, forever merging" must also come to such, sadness increasing, and at Shiogama Beach a bell sounded evening. A *samidare* sky cleared some, faint early moon, Magaki Island also coming clear. "Fishing boats" pulling together, voices dividing the catch, "the haul's excitement" grasped now, rousing deep response. That night a blind minstrel played *biwa* and chanted *Oku-jōruri*. Not like Tales of the Heike nor *mai*, singing country tunes boisterously to our pillows, but not unusual either, traditional in such out-of-the-way places, and good they're kept up.

(May 9)

25

Early morning visited Shiogama Myōjin shrine. The *kokushu* had had it rebuilt, pillars immense, painted rafters resplendent, stone steps rising rather steeply, morning sun blazing vermillion-lacquered fence. As far as the road goes, to the very end of dusty earth, the unimaginable power of the gods persists and still answers each need, one of our country's traditions and to my mind most precious. Before the shrine a fine old lantern. On its metal door the inscription read:

IN THE THIRD YEAR OF THE BUNJI
CONTRIBUTED BY IZUMI SABURŌ

(1187)

Images of five centuries floated before my eyes, making me feel, despite myself, strange. Here was a courageous loyal trustworthy warrior. To this day no one's not revered his name. Yes, man should follow the way of jen and stick to his principles. As they say, fame will follow, in turn, of itself.

26

Sun almost at height already. Hired boat and crossed to Matsushima. Distance of more than two *li*. Landed at Ojima Beach.

Now, though it's been only too often observed, Matsushima presents a magnificent vista, the finest in our "mulberry land" and comparable to that of Lake Dotei or Seiko. The sea enters at the southeast, three *li* wide at that point, like Sekko at flood tide. All sorts of islands gather here, steep ones pointing to sky, others creeping upon waves. Or some piled double on each other, or even triple, and some divided at one end and overlapping at the other. Some bear others on their backs, some seem to embrace them, as if caressing their offspring. Green of the pines deep, needles and branches mauled by the salt winds—though contorted by nature—look artificially trained. The feeling: one of intense beauty, or a lovely creature engrossed in her glass. Perhaps in the Age of the Gods Ōyamazumi shaped this place. Who with brush or speech can hope to describe the work of heaven and earth's divinity?

(May 9)

27

Ojima Beach, connected to mainland, projects into the sea. There, ruins of Ungozenji's hut and *zazen* rock and other things remain. And there too amongst pines still seen religious recluses, several here and there, by thatched huts where twigs drop off, living quietly, it seemed, as smoke of leaves and pine-cones rose. And though unknown to me, they drew my heart/mind, moon now mirrored in sea, the day's view altered, renewed. Back on shore, put up at inn whose second-story windows opened upon sea, feeling of resting on the journey now among wind and cloud, extraordinarily high.

> Matsushima
> come in the guise of a crane
> *hototogisu*
>> (Sora)

I, wordless, tried sleeping, but couldn't. On leaving my old hut Sodō had made me a poem about Matsushima. And Hara Anteki a *waka* about Matsu-ga-urashima. Undid my neckbag, let them be my company this night. And with them *hokku* from Sampū and Dakushi.

28

On the eleventh visited Zuiganji. This temple founded some thirty-two generations ago when Makabe-no-Heishiro entered the priesthood, upon returning from Tō. Later, influenced by Ungozenji's superior character, the seven main buildings, tiles newly refurbished, walls gilded, splendidly embellished, seem to have become the great edifice of the arrived-at Buddha land. Wondered if temple of Kenbutsu Hijiri might also be seen.

(May 11)

29

On the twelfth setting out for Hiraizumi via the celebrated Pine of Aneha and the Odae Bridge, found ourselves pursuing a path with few signs of life, only an occasional hunter or woodcutter passing, ended up, after wrong turn-off, at harbor-town called Ishi-no-maki. Mt. Kinka, described in a poem to an emperor as "where gold blossoms," seen far over water and hundreds of cargo boats clustering inlet, human dwellings there contesting space, smoke curling up from ovens. Our unexpected arrival prompted immediate effort to procure lodgings, but nothing to be had. In the end found a corner in a shack for that night and at daybreak off again on unknown paths. Saw Sode Ferry, Obuchi Meadows, Mano Reedflats from afar, following along a long embankment. Bypassed a dismal stretch of marshland and spent night at place called Toima and finally reached Hiraizumi. Distance covered, roughly, more than twenty *li*.

(May 12-13)

Magnificence of three generations "gone as in a sleep" and shambles of great outer gate one *li* this side of what was. Where Hidehira's seat was, now largely empty fields and only Mt. Kinkei unchanged. Climbing to Takadachi discovered the Kitakami a large stream flowing from region of Nambu. The Koromogawa, encircling Izumi Castle, below Takadachi, empties into the larger stream. The ancient ruins of Yasuhira and others, with the Koromo Barrier between fortifying entrance into Nambu, seem to have guarded against Ezo people. For all that, the faithful retainers, the elite, were confined to the castle, their moment of valiant effort so much grass. "The country devastated, mountains and rivers remain; in the castle in spring the grass green" remembered and we set our hats under us and sat there for a time and tears came.

> the summer grasses
> the mightiest warriors'
> dreams' consequences
>
> in *unohana*
> Kanefusa appearing
> white-headed alas
>
> (Sora)

Two temple halls we'd heard of, open. The *kyōdō* contains images of the Three Generals and the *hikarido* coffins of the three generations and enshrines the three images of Buddha. The Seven Gems now gone, jewelled doors rent by winds, gilded pillars fretted by frost and snow, would have all been long since destroyed and back to grass but for reinforced walls on four sides and a cover over the tiled roof against wind and rain. So it still stands, memorial of a thousand years past.

> the rains of summer
> in falling may have left ah
> *hikaridō*

31

Seeing Nambu Road a good ways off, stayed over at village of Iwade. Went on via Ogurozaki, Mizu-no-ojima, and from Narugo Hot Springs made for the Shitomae Barrier and on over into province of Dewa. This route few travellers ever take, so guards eyed us suspiciously and barely let us through. Climbed high mountain there, sun already down, and happening on a border-guard hut sought shelter there. For three days winds and rain fierce, forced to hang on in that dull retreat.

> what with fleas and lice
> the horse's having a piss
> right at the pillow

(May 15)

32

Man at the hut said, "From here to Dewa, with a high mountain to cross and the trail far from clear, better get a guide to take you over." So we hired a man, a strapping young fellow who looked like he could take care of himself, with curved short-sword at hip and oaken staff in hand, and on he took us. Felt like just the day to sort with danger and with some fear followed after. As the man said, the mountain was high and thickly wooded, beyond bird cry, in deep forest darkness like groping about at night. Felt as if dirt were tumbling from overloaded clouds, pushed pushed on through *shino* brush, waded water, stumbled rock, drenched in cold sweat, came out at last in region of Mogami. Our guide then said, "Generally it's not so easy along this trail. Glad we made it this time without any adventures." And contentedly left us. But we, even hearing this afterwards, found our hearts beating faster.

(May 17)

33

At Obanazawa visited man called Seifū. Well-to-do but not a petty mind. And from frequent trips to Miyako well appreciates how wayfarers feel, had us stay many days to rest up after being so much on the go, entertained us in a host of ways.

so nice and cool
making myself right at home
sprawled out for a nap

hey come on out you
from under the silkworm room
with the croaking voice

the eyebrow brush
so putting one in mind of
the safflower

silkworm attending
people from antiquity
in their appearance
                    (Sora)

(May 17-26)

34

In the demesne of Yamagata the mountain temple called Ryūshakuji. Founded by Jikaku Daishi, unusually well-kept quiet place. "You must go and see it," people urged; from here, off back toward Obanazawa, about seven *li*. Sun not yet down. Reserved space at dormitory at bottom, then climbed to temple on ridge. This mountain one of rocky steeps, ancient pines and cypresses, old earth and stone and smooth moss, and on the rocks temple-doors locked, no sound. Climbed along edges of and crept over boulders, worshipped at temples, penetrating scene, profound quietness, heart/mind open clear.

> silence itself is
> in the rock absorbing
> cicada sounds

(May 27)

35

Intending to ride down the Mogamigawa, waited at a place called Ōishida for good weather. Here the seeds of old *haikai* sown, brought back past times and unforgotten flowers, cry of a reed-flute easing heart, gone astray trying to take both ways at once, the new and the old, no one to guide them, left them a collection of no great merit. But as far as *furyu* had till then come.

The Mogamigawa has its source in Michinoku and its upper reaches in Yamagata. With the daunting perils of the Goten shoals and Hayabusa rapids. Descending north of Mt. Itajiki, it empties into sea at Sakata. Right, left, mountains close, up, boat shot down through clustering trees. Boats like this with sheaves of rice probably those called *inafune*. The Shiraito Falls plunges through thick green foliage and the Sennindo stands at river's brink. What with swollen waters, boat ran risks.

> the rains of summer
> gathering rapidly to
> Mogamigawa

(May 28)

42

36

Third day of the sixth moon, climbed Haguroyama. Visited Zushi Sakichi and received in audience by the *betto-dai*, Egaku Ajari. Lodged at side-temple at Minamidani and he eagerly and cordially welcomed us.

The fourth, at main temple building, *haikai* party.

> thank *you* very much
> for all your perfuming snow
> Minamidani

On the fifth worshipped at Gongen temple. Its founder, Nōjo Daishi, but date unknown. In the *Engishiki* given as shrine of Ushusatoyama. Whoever did the copying wrote "satoyama" for "kuro," by mistake probably. One of the Ushūkuroyama *kanji* dropped out and so it became Hagurogama probably. The idea of Dewa seems clarified in the *Fudoki*, where payments in down and feathers are mentioned as a form of local tribute. Gassan and Yudono with it compose a trinity. This temple affiliated with Tōei in Bukō, the moon of the Tendai *shi-kan* clear, way of *endonyuzu*, light increased, ridge to temple ridge extending, the devout encouraging each other in austere duties, the grace revealed (*genko*) in heart's mountains and heart's land calls forth reverence and awe in folk. Prosperity unconfined and the mountains may be said to bestow blessings.

(June 3)

Eighth, climbed Gassan. Yūshime hanging from our necks, heads covered by *hōkan*, led by a *goriki*, up into mountain air, clouds, mist, walking ice and snow, going some eight *li* up until it seemed near the gateway to the clouds, sun and moon passing over, each breath a last one, numb, reached peak, sun down, moon out. Spread bamboo grass, used shino as pillows, lay down, waited for daybreak. Sun up, clouds gone, headed down toward Yudono.

At valley's edge place known as the Swordsmiths' Hut. Smiths in these parts fetch holy water here to purify themselves and to temper blades in which they eventually carve: Gassan: a mark of wide repute. Said that swords were tempered at the Ryusen too. Reminiscent of ancient Kansho and Bakuya. That their dedication to their craft not superficial, well-known. Perched on rock resting a while, saw half-opened buds of three-foot cherry trees. Buried under piled-up reluctant snow, slow blossoms don't forget spring, remarkable stubbornness. As if the "plum under blazing heaven" were suddenly seen here. Recalled Gyōson Sōjō's poem, which made buds seem to bud the more. By and large against code to disclose what goes on here. And with that the brush stops, won't write. Went back to dormitory and at the Ajari's instance wrote poems of our visit to the Three Mountains on *tanzaku*.

> coolness itself ah
> the dimlit three day crescent's
> Haguro-san

> the summits of clouds
> but how many giving way
> to the moon's mountain

> prohibited speech
> at Yudono moistening
> the edge of a sleeve

> Yudono-yama
> pennies for the stepping-stones
> and many a tear
>
> (Sora)

(June 8)

38

Left Haguro and at castle town of Tsuru-ga-oka received by Nagayama Shigeyuki at his place and composed a round of *haikai* there. Sakichi, who had come this far, saw us off. Went by river-boat down to harbor of Sakata. Stayed at the doctor En-an Fugyoku's house.

from Mount Atsumi
over to Fuku-ura
the evening's cooling

a sticky sun
into the vast sea driven
Mogamigawa

(June 13)

45

39

After countless displays of rivers and mountains, land and sea, for eyes, the heart's inch-space now bounded towards Kisakata. From Sakata harbor north-east, crossing mountains, following shore, walking sand, some ten *li*, sun falling, sea wind swirling grit, gusty rain hid Mt. Chōkai. Groping through darkness, maybe rain "an enchantment" anyhow and later clearing like a charm, maybe, and so squeezed into a fisherman's shanty to wait till the wet let up. Next morning, sky utterly clear, sun miraculous, dazzling, boated about Kisakata. First headed for Nōin Island, prayed at what of his three years' retreat remains, then over to opposite shore and found the old cherry tree—"over whose blossoms [fishermen] row"—memorializing Saigyō-Hoshi. At water's edge an imperial tomb said to be Jingū Kogu's. Temple there known as Kanmanjuji. Never heard of Empress visiting it. How come?

Sitting in temple *hojo*, rolling up blinds, eyes held the scene: to south Chōkai supporting heaven, its image resting in water.

West the Muyamuya Barrier obstructs and east along a builtup embankment, road to Akita far off, sea to north sheltering, and just where the tide rolls in, place called Shiogoshi.

(June 16)

46

From one end to other and out again bay's about a *li*, superficially resembling Matsushima, but with a certain difference. Matsushima seems to smile, whereas Kisakata seems aggrieved. Tinge of the sad in its isolatedness, nature here like a troubled spirit.

> Kisakata
> in the rain a Seishi
> silk-tree sleep blossom

> Shiogoshi
> legs of a crane dripping
> from the ocean freshness

> (The Festival)
> Kisakata
> whatever there is for food
> is a divine feast
>
> (Sora)

> a fisherman's home
> the shutters taken out in
> to the evening's cool
>
> (Teiji Merchant of Mino)

> (On Finding an Osprey Nest on a Rock)
> waves do not undo
> the vow that was pledged
> at the osprey's nest
>
> (*Sora*)

40

Reluctantly left Sakata, days piling up, seeing clouds above the Hokuroku district. Mind aches, the distance, hearing it's a hundred and thirty *li* to Kaga City. Crossed the Nezu Barrier, starting fresh into Echigo, reached the Ichiburi Barrier in Etchu. During this stretch of nine days putting up with heat and rain, spirit sore afflicted, taken ill, no way to keep up writing.

> On the sixth day of
> even this month's poetry's
> night unusual
>
> rough as the sea is
> reaching over to Sado
> the Heaven's star stream

(June 25)

41

     Today making our way past Oyashirazu, Koshirazu, Inumodori and Komagaeshi, amongst the most dangerous spots in Hokkoku and named accordingly, worn out by it, pulled up pillows and bedded down for night, only to catch sounds of voices in front room one room away, sounding like two young women. Old man's voice mingled with theirs as stories told are heard and it seemed they were play-girls from Niigata in Echigo Province. On their way to the Ise Shrines and the man seeing them off as far as the Barrier, heading back next morning with notes of theirs and usual greetings home. " 'On the strand where white waves crash' we wander, children of the sea, thus fallen, to every chance relation, every day *karma*, shame . . .," heard tearfully, saying: "We don't know which way we're supposed to go and feel so uncertain and helpless, could we just follow in sight of your footsteps. By the grace of your robes, please grant us the blessing of your mercy and the providence of Buddha." "Unfortunately we often like to take detours. Just follow anyone going your way. Surely the gods will protect you and see you safely through," words lift them on leaving, but felt sorry for them for some time after.

> in the same house
> girls of pleasure also slept
> *hagi* and moonlight

Sora hearing this wrote it down.

42

The Kurobe known for its forty-eight rapids and we did have to cross no end of water-ways to get to bay called Nago. Though not spring and feeling, in fact, of early fall pervasive, waves of wisteria at Tako suggested a visit and asking the way were told: "From here it's five *li* along the coast, then over the mountain there—not much more than a handful of fishermen's huts, a night's lodging even in the reeds hard to find," enough to scare us off; so on into province of Kaga.

> early rice fragrance
> making its way to the right
> into the "Rough Sea"

(July 14)

43

Crossed Mt. Unohana and Vale of Kurikara, in Kanazawa on mid-fifth of the seventh moon. Kasho, a merchant from Osaka, in town. Stayed at same inn. One Issho, known for his devotion to the art, of some repute too in the world outside, died unexpectedly this past winter quite young and his elder brother was now conducting memorial services:

> tomb you also move
> my own voice's lamenting
> the autumnal winds

On being invited to a thatched hermitage:

> the autumn coolness
> hand and hand paring away
> eggplants cucumbers

And on the road this poem:

> scarlet on scarlet
> the sun unrelentingly
> the autumn winds

(July 15)

44

At a place called Komatsu:

with such modesty
the name Komatsu breathing
hagi/susuki

Visited Tada Shrine here. Sanemori's helmet and part of its *nishiki* there. In days of old, presented to him, as a member of the Genji, by his commander Yoshitomo, it is said. Clearly not designed for a common soldier. From eye-cover to earflap engraved with chrysanthemums interlaced by ivy scrollwork, a dragon headpiece with hoe-shaped frontlets attached. After Sanemori's death in battle, Kiso Yoshinaka with message of prayer donated it to shrine, Higochi Jirō his emissary: can see them there even now as annals of shrine describe.

merciless indeed
under the ancient helmet
a cricket crickets

(July 25)

53

45

On the way to hot springs at Yamanaka saw as we went Mt. Shirane just behind. At foot of mountain to left a Kannondo. The retired Emperor Kazan, after pilgrimage to the Thirty-Three Temples, had an image of Daiji Daihi enshrined here and named the place Nata, it is said. The name, it is also said, comes from *kanji* taken from Nachi and Tanigumi. All kinds of odd-shaped rocks abound and ancient pines amongst them; small *kaya*-thatched temple there, handsomely situated.

> Ishiyama's
> stones no whiter than
> the autumn winds

46

       Bathed at the hot springs. Their efficacy said to be nearly up to Ariake's.

> Yamanaka
> leave chrysanthemums unplucked
> redolent water

Our host here, known as Kumenosuke, a mere lad, whose father doted on *haikai* and who so embarrassed Teishitsu of Raku when he visited here as a young man at the art that when he returned to Raku he became a disciple of Teitoku and thus gained renown. Because of the earlier occasion, however, when he later came as judge, they say, he refused payment here. This has already become legend.

    Sora, stomach ailing, went off to relatives at Nagashima in Ise, writing down:

> walking on and on
> though feeling painfully sick
> through fields of *hagi*

Pain of one who goes, emptiness of one left behind, like the parting of a pair of wild geese, lost in clouds. And I too:

> from this very day
> cancel out the inscription
> bamboo peaked hat's dew

(July 27–August 5 or 6)

47

Stayed just outside the castle town of Daishōji at the Zenshōji.
Still in Kaga country. Sora at this temple only last night and left here:

> all that night
> the autumn winds being heard
> beyond the mountains

A single night feels like a thousand *li*. I heard fall winds too, resting in temple dormitory, and towards daybreak voices chanting sutras clearer, gongs, and went to refectory. Today had to be off into Echizen country and with that in mind hurrying from the temple, young priests came hurrying down the steps after me with paper and ink-slab. At that moment willows in the yard were shedding leaves:

> sweeping the garden
> but letting the temple keep
> the willows' droppings

Sandals already on, jotted it hastily down for them.

48

At boundary of Echizen, inlet of Yoshizaki, hired a boat there for the pines of Shiogoshi.

> throughout the long night
> the violence of the waves
> bearing all along
> making the very moon drip
> the pines of Shiogoshi

In this one poem are the various feelings of the place expressed. To add to it would be just pointing one finger too many.

(August 10?)

49

Visited the venerable elder of Tendryūji at Maruoka, renewing old acquaintances. And Hokushi from Kanazawa also, who'd—as it happened—seen me this far and now reluctantly turned back. His way of mulling and noting what eyes see of various places often quite sensitive, now facing departure:

> what was created
> on the fan and prized apart
> subsides together

Went off fifty *cho* into mountains to pray at Eiheiji, Dōgenzenji's temple. To have situated it beyond such mountains "a thousand *li* from Hoki" was, as they say, the result of careful consideration.

August 11?)

50

Fukui about three *li* from here and after supper struck out for it, the way as darkness came on no mean trick for feet. Old recluse called Tōsai living here. When was it he came to call on me in Edo? More than ten years already. Has he turned senile now or is he dead? Told upon enquiring: "Still alive," living at such and such a place. Quiet spot off the road a piece, modest weather-beaten house, all entangled in *yugao* and *hechima* and the door lost behind *keitō* and *hahakigi*. Well, this must be it, and knocked at door, bringing a humble woman out. "Where does the reverend *gobō* come from? The master of the house has gone to Mr. So-and-so's, not far from here. if you want him, please look for him there," she said; seemed to be his wife. Looking like someone straight out of legend, and at once went off after him, found him and stayed two nights at their house, leaving again then for the full moon at Tsuruga harbor. Tōsai, tucking up his *kimono* in a funny sort of way, cheerfully decided to come along and serve as a guidepost.

(August 11–12 or 12–13?

51

As time passed, Mt. Shirane vanished, Mt. Hina emerged. Crossed the Asamuzu Bridge, the reeds at Tamae flourishing, through the Uguisu Barrier, via the Yuno-o Pass, the Castle of Hiuchi, at Mt. Kaeru heard first wild geese cry, and on evening of the fourteenth at Tsuruga harbor found lodging at inn. That night the moon especially bright. "Think it'll be like this tomorrow night?" "Hard to tell about weather in Koshiji. Might be fine and then again might be overcast," and after some *sake* from innkeeper, paid night visit to the Kehi Myōjin. Monument to Emperor Chūai. Certain solemnity about shrine, moon through pines touched white sand before edifice as if with frost. In days of old Yūgyo Shōnin the 2nd undertook the immense project of making access for visitors much easier, himself helped cut grass, lug earth and rocks, drain marshes. Nor has the old custom yet stopped and sand is still carried to shrine. "Known as *Yūgyo-no-sunamochi*," innkeeper explained.

> the moon pure and clear
> Yugyo carried carrying
> sand to cover up

The fifteenth, just as innkeeper predicted, it rains.

> here's the harvest moon
> good old Hokkoku weather
> don't depend on it

(August 14)

52

Sixteenth, sky clearing, decided to gather small shells, sailed along Iro Beach. Altogether seven *li*. One Tenya So-and-so, with carefully-packed *warigo* and *sasae*, etc., taking servants along for the ride, enjoying tailwinds arrived in good time. Only a few fishermen's huts along beach and bedraggled Hokke temple nearby. Here drank tea, hot *sake*, much moved by the pervading sense of isolatedness at nightfall.

> isolation's more
> overwhelming than Suma
> beach's autumntide

> between wave and wave
> a confusion of small shells
> the *hagi's* jetsam

Had Tōsai take the brush and set down major events of the day, to leave at the temple.

53

Rotsū had come to the harbor to meet me and came along into Mino. Reached the demesne of Ōgaki by horse, Sora having also come in from Ise and Etsujin come galloping in, got together at Jokō's house. Zensenshi, Keikō father and sons, as well as other friends, day and night, kindly called, as if encountering someone restored to life, showing their pleasure and warm affection. Before fully recovering from the exhaustion and exertion of the long journey, on the sixth day of *Nagatsuki*, decided to visit the ceremonial rebuilding at Ise, back in the boat again,

> the *hamaguri*
> shell and innards in parting
> departing fall so.

(September 3–6?)

EPILOGUE

The dry tone and rich, supple, vigorous style keep me immersed in reading the *Oku-no-hosomichi*, sometimes arising and clapping or lying down, stirred to the core. Once had my raincoat on, eager to go on a like journey, and then again content to sit imaging those rare sights. What a hoard of feelings, Kojin jewels, has his brush depicted! Such a journey! Such a man! A pity only that he turns wearier and more and more white comes tingeing his brows.

written by Soryū
(early summer, seventh year of the Genroku)

NOTES

The biography of Bashō (1644-94) is available most succinctly and accurately, as far as it goes, in *Haikai* and *Haiku*, published by the Nippon Gakujutsu Shinkokai, Tokyo, in 1958. And all the various terms relating to *haiku* are adequately explained in the same volume. There is no lack of books on the subject in English now, in any event, and the interested reader will have no trouble finding information. Enough to note here that the *Oku-no-hosomichi* is the last of the travel journals and regarded as the most mature of them. Bashō was, as a youngster, in the service of a feudal lord, chiefly as attendant to the lord's son (Todo Yoshitada), who died unfortunately—though perhaps fortunately for us—at the age of twenty-two. This led to Bashō's removing himself boldly from the Yoshitada household and into a much more independent life. He had already been attracted to poetry as well as to contemplative religion. First living in Kyoto, till about age twenty-eight, thereafter—apart from journeys—largely in Edo (Tokyo). His pen-name (family name Matsuo), Bashō, was drawn from the plantain tree near the hut he lived in—about age thirty-seven—provided him by Sampū. Evidently the tree's "usefulness" (in a manner reminiscent of Taoism) was the key factor in leading to his taking the name.

The travel journal was a well-established Oriental tradition. By the time Bashō was ready to compose the *Oku-no-hosomichi* he had become very aware of its possibilities. He projects with unusual economy of force the fullness of his life and sensibility, and the resonance of that life and sensibility reaches us yet.

The original text, the Soryū version, is unpunctuated, though there are natural clear syntactic units. Bashō's syntax, however, though often frowned upon by latterday Japanese grammarians for its lack of rule, is curious, characteristic, and exact. We have tried not to improve upon it.

The notes could be hopelessly voluminous. We have preferred to offer only what additional word is immediately illuminating or stimulating, and a few points are elaborated to give some sense of a depth involved throughout that might not otherwise be fully realized. The reader may assume that when Bashō uses "standard locutions" (like brushing the cobwebs off his hut) he does so for a sense of relation with past literary usage and for the concrete values he feels anew. Allusions are everywhere, often in single words. They were not as remote as, say, those in *The Wasteland* are to most of us. They were expected to be grasped at once by any likely reader of that time: no one was expected to apply to an encyclopedia or thesaurus. Certain key anthologies—notably the *Wakanroeishu*, half of which was Chinese classical poetry—were highly popular with the middle classes and certainly much poetry was current and remembered.

It may be worth reminding the reader that Bashō didn't, in effect, *write* poetry, but made it—spoke it, aired it. *Haiku* were easily carried in the head the formalities of the structure (and you see Japanese today ticking off the syllables as they try to recall some) were a great help. Bashō wasn't, in short, sitting at a desk writing. The poems were made often on the spur of the moment and for specific occasions. By the time they were incorporated in works like this one, of course, they had undergone revision. Certainly reconsideration. And Bashō, conscientious as always and with more at stake than his followers, would not have inserted any work that seemed to him inferior. It follows, then, that the poems by Sora and others are well-regarded by the master, providing thematic counterpoint and accompaniment, and not for the sake of making Bashō's poems look better.

Samuel Johnson has noted (in his *Preface to Shakespeare*, 1765) "Parts are not to be examined till the whole has been surveyed; there is a kind of intellectual remoteness necessary for the comprehension of any great work in its full design and in its true proportions; a close approach shows the smaller niceties, but the beauty of the whole is discerned no longer."

TITLE

The title of the journal: The *Oku-no-hosomichi*, literally means: Oku's Narrow Path(s). Oku is the region north and west of Edo (Tokyo). In Bashō's day it was considered rather remote and off the beaten track. But the Narrow Path also refers to a specific road that travellers generally followed in passing through the region. The word "strait" may be more apt than "narrow." The title suggests to the Japanese mind the deep and difficult way. The way through life. The *selva oscura*, perhaps.

Cf. Bruno Snell: *Discovery of the Mind*, p. 304—"Callimachus was the first to introduce the proud rejection of vulgarity into poetry. We now know this chiefly from the prologue to the Aitia. He does not want to travel on the broad highway thronged by others, but on his own path, however narrow."

INTRODUCTION

"*When tears come...:*" cf. Leopardi's letter (of 20 Feb. 1823): "I went to visit the tomb of Tasso and wept there. This is the first and only *pleasure* I have felt in Rome...." A contemporary poet, an American traveling in the traditional scenes of Europe (Louis Zutofsky, *Four Other Countries* (1956-57), writes: " ...Liveable/place; whose character is/endurable// As the eyes are moist before/the regularly spaced/flower window boxes/ of Berne...," and cf. in Lévi-Strauss's (Eng. *The Savage Mind*) quote of T.G.H. Strehlow: "The Northern Aranda (Australia) clings to his native soil with every fibre of his being. He will always speak of his own 'birthplace' with love and reverence. Today, tears will come into his eyes when he mentions an ancestral home site.... Mountains and creeks and springs and water-holes are, to him, not merely interesting or beautiful scenic features...; they are the handiwork of ancestors from whom he himself has descended.... The whole countryside is his living, age-old family tree...."

1

Moon & Sun...: The opening words allude to writing of Li Po (701-62). Often translated as "Months and days..." (which the words also mean, but these terms seem inadequate. Dr. D.T. Suzuki shares our opinion. It may not be irrelevant to point out that Plato in the *Timaeus* (38 C ff.) in referring to the revolvings of moon and sun mentions that the word *planet* (a Greek word) means "wanderer." And Leopardi a century or more after Bashō could see the moon also as a "wandering" figure.

many that perished: Bashō has in mind his favorites, Saigyō (1118-90), itinerant priest-poet famous for his *waka* (in *Shinkokinshū:* Kamakura anthology), whose trail Bashō largely follows; Sōgi (1421-1502), priest-poet noted for work in *renka*, and a major influence on Bashō; the Chinese poets Li Po and Tu Fu—like most T'ang poets in government service "on the road." The reader should understand that Bashō's health at the outset has been on the wane, so that his speculation about dying on the journey is not idle, nor romantic. And the fact that the journal was composed *afterwards*, when Bashō's health was even more clearly declining, aware that he *didn't* die on the journey, underlines the aches involved, quietly. Out of the worst Bashō will make the best.

Barrier (Japanese *seki*): These were border checkpoints, mounted by guards. Already identification papers (so common were political incursions) were the order of the day in Japan and had been for some centuries past. Pilgrims and itinerant actors usually had an easier going of it, but were also natural disguises.

Dōsojin: Japanese counterpart of Hermes. God of wayfarers, with carved stone markers at roadsides, bridges, etc. Against diseases and/or evil spirits. Also divine link between living and dead.

momohiki: Light cotton britches

kasa: peaked sedge or bamboo rain and sun hat

Sampū (1647-1732): Patron and disciple of Bashō. Wealthy fish-merchant. Sampū's summer house, it may be noted, was only 500 yards or so from the earlier dwelling. Any man of means in the Edo area would provide himself with several homes for reasons as practical as frequent fires and mistresses.

the grass door: The poem is evidently expressing, under the general theme of transiency, a proportion that read: "Matsushima is to Sampū's summer house as that was to the 'grass door' hut." The "dolls' house" provides a clear seasonal note of the *Hina matsuri* (Girls' Festival, held on March 3) when dolls, usually of imperial proportions, are carefully posted in tiers on an altar.

omote: opening page of a *renka* (linked verses).

2

Yayoi: Old term for March, literally "time for growing." All the old lunar names have exact relation to rice-farming, the growing of this Japanese foodstuff being a constant of the landscape.

"a waning moon...": From the Hahakigi section of the *Genji Monogatari*

Senju: A well-known jumping-off point on the road to Oku and a fishing center at the confluence of streams just north of Edo.

li: Chinese measure, about 2.5 miles.

departing spring: The poem, apart from its allusion to Chinese poetry, suggests Sampū, the fish merchant, who must have been among the company bidding the travelers farewell (there would have been a party of sorts), and the "birds" suggest the wanderers-to-be.

fishes'/eyes tears: Alluding to a poem by Tu Fu (712-70), as does the exaggerated sense of distance preceding.

yatate: Portable brush and sumi ink kit.

3

Genroku (1688-1703): Tokugawa shōgunate. Time of relative freedom and well-being in Japan, at least in the centers. Cf. Saikaku, Chikamatsu, and the flourishing art of *ukiyo-e*.

Ōü: variant of Oku.

"*under Go skies*": Go is Japanese reading of Chinese *Wu*; remote area evoking images of snow and old age. Linked to poetry by Po Chü-i (772–846) or Li Tung (end of 9th century). (Achilles Fang)

kamiko: Strong paper clothing

yukata: Light summer clothing

hanamuke: Farewell gifts. Johnson in *A Journey to the Western Islands* (1773-5) writes, "It is not to be imagined without experience, how in climbing crags, and treading bogs, and winding through narrow and obstructed passages, a little bulk will hinder, and a little weight will burthen; or how often a man that has pleased himself at home with his own resolution, will, in the hour of darkness and fatigue, be content to leave behind him everything but himself."

4

Konahana Sakuya Hime: Legendary princess; lit., "princess who causes flowers to bloom." Daughter of Oyamatsumi-no-kami, the mountain god. To prove, although pregnant, she was not unfaithful to her newly-wed divine husband, Prince Ninigi, she sealed herself in the Utsumuro (exitless room) and set fire to it. Out of this ordeal Prince Hohodemi was born, the name meaning "appearing out of fire."

konoshiro: *Konosius punctalus*, fish of about seven to eight inch length generally, found mostly in the Inland Sea today. When burnt, it has the odor of a cremated body and was substituted for a girl once in a rather similar fix to our princess (cf. Iphigeneia in Taurus). Literally the word means "in place of a child."

5

Nikkō: Also read Nikōzan, literally, "sunlight."

Hotoke Gozaemon: Like saying, "Jack Buddha."

jen: Confucian term. Cf. Pound's version of the *Analects*. Relating analogously: *vir* and *virtu*, i.e., manfulness, clear-spirited, etc.

6

Uzuki: Literally, "month of the U flower."

Futarayama: Literally, "Two Wastes Mountain."

Kūkai Daishi (774 or 5–834 or 5): Sometimes known as Kōbō Daishi, founder of Shingon sect (Buddhist). High priest famous for calligraphy (said to have invented *hiragana syllabary*), poetry, and religious works.

eight directions: The eight major compass points. cf. Waley's version of a poem by T'ao Chien (*Chinese Poems*, p. 107): "The lingering clouds, rolling, rolling/And the settled rain, dripping,/In the Eight Directions— the same dusk.... "

the four classes: Under feudal rule: warrior, farmer, artisan, merchant.

7

Mt.: In this journal and generally, the word "yama" is translated "mountain" or "mount," though often the Western eye would say "hill." The feeling, however, is in terms of local scale, and mountain is more apt.

Kurokami: Literally, "black hair."

changing apparel: In lunar reckoning seasonal changes of clothing customarily occurred on April 1st and October 1st. In *haikai* the reference is to spring. As for name-changing, even today it's done by some priests and artists. Sōgō means "the enlightened."

Sora (1649–1710): About 1689, definitively affiliated with Bashō. His poems tend to be much slighter than Bashō's, but clearly felt and point particularities. Sora is his pen-name, not his actual given name.

bashō: The plantain tree.

chō: About 200 yards.

shaku: Almost precisely equal to our foot, twelve inches.

Urami: Literally, "back view."

to a waterfall confined: Religious ascetics frequently used to stand immersed in a waterfall as an "exercise" in late spring/early summer.

8

kasane: As explained in poem, the flower's name and a curious, but attractive, rural-type name. Cf. our "daisy" or "myrtle."

9

kandai: Castle overseer.

Inuoümono: This refers to a sport indulged in by warriors of Heian and Kamakura times. Dogs, corralled by bamboo fencing, were shot at by warriors riding by with bow and arrow. A form of archery practice gone out of fashion as missiles and targets have improved.

Tamamo-no-mae: Japan's (via China) famous fox-lady (we only have "vixens"). The details of her story are told in the Nôh, *Sesshôseki*; "-mae," is a feminine honorific, like "lady."

Shô-hachiman: Warrior deity, with shrines found in various parts of Japan.

Yoichi: One of Minamoto Yoshitsune's (of the Genji) heroic warriors. The story is told in the *Heike Monogatari*: an incident at the battle of Yashima of unusual prowess in archery.

Shugen-Kômyôji: the reader will realize that the ending *ji* in such place names refers to "temple," as *yama* or *san* means mountain or mount; *gawa* is river or stream.

gyôjadô: Hall for *yamabushi* priest austerities.

ashida: High rain clogs. Here likely referring specifically to those kept on an altar at the shrine and considered En-no-gyôja's (founder of Shugendô sect; i.e., religious asceticism, *yamabushi* tribe). They would be worshipped as strength-giving in the art of long-distance walking.

10

Butchô-oshô: (1641-1715), Bashô's Zen master.

-oshô: Bashô uses religious titles for individuals which are untranslatable into Christian terms. We have preferred to keep them and so at least cue the reader to distinctions.

Hôshi: Bonze (Dharma master).

the ten views: A way of saying "having wandered about the temple precincts (landscaped gardens)": five bridges, ten views is the landscaping formula.

Myôzenji or Genmyôzenji (1239-1296): *Zenji*: Chinese ch'an-shih. Ch'an (Zen) master who lived fifteen years in a secluded cave, much sought out for teachings. Cave-names, given by the dwellers themselves, remain suggestive.

Hôun-Hôshi (467-529): In Chinese, *Fa-yün Fa-shih*. Chinese high priest, who toward end of his life built a hermitage in or against a rock-cave, where disciples arrived for chatter.

11

Sesshōseki: Still exists, though fenced about. The legends associated with it are told in Nōh of the same name.

tanzaku: Narrow strip of fine paper to write poetry on; a poem.

hototogisu: Japanese cuckoo, whose name is its song.

12

willow of the "pacing stream": Refers to a *waka* by Saigyō; cf. Nōh play *Yugyōyanagi,* which also touches on the Shirakawa Barrier in the next section.

gunshu: Feudal deputy governor.

13

"somehow sending word...:" Quote from a *waka* by Taira Kanemori.

Miyako: The capital, usually Kyoto in old poetry; here Bashō would mean Edo.

Three Barriers: Variously identified, but the Shirakawa-seki most often in poetry. *"Autumnal winds":* from a *waka* by Nōin-Hōshi; *"the maple"* from a *waka* by Yorimasa.

unohana: Deutzia scabra; small white flowers.

Kiyosuke (1104–1177): Of the Fujiwara. Late Heian poet. Referring to Takeda Kuniyuki's donning court robes at the Barrier in deference to the poem by Nōin mentioned above. Cf. Jouvenel, *Sovereignty,* p. 103: "Investiture...consists in clothing a man anew in robes which are at once pure and majestic."

kanmuri: Small black formal hat, held in place by a pin.

Sora's haiku: Gaily alludes to all that precedes.

14

Kagenuma: Shadow Pond or Mirror Pond.

Tōkyū: (1638–1715). The local *haikai* man. Six years older than Bashō. Had met in Edo. Much revered in his area.

fūryū: Literally, "wind-fluent," this untranslatable term is defined by Bashō's uses of it in this journal. Reflective of Japanese taste for the natural, immediate, and humble, as well as evanescent, as graceful.

waki and daisan: Renka terms. The opening 5-7-5 syllable poem in a *renka* is the *hokku;* the second 7-7 syllable poem is the *waki* (cf. *waki* role, sidekick, in Nōh); and the third 7-7 syllable poem the *daisan*.

15

"in mountain depths....": Alluding to a poem by Saigyō. Cf. *Chuang-tzu*, Bk. 24, v. 14.

kanji: Chinese ideogram.

the Western Paradise: Buddhist allusion, locale of Amitabha (the Measureless Light), one of the great Buddhist incarnations.

Gyōgi Bosatsu (668 or 670–749): High priest in the Nara period, Korean by birth (cf. Chapter 8, *Japanese Buddhism*, Sir Charles Eliot). *Bosatsu* (Boddhisattva) is an honorary title conferred upon him by the Emperor Shōmu (724–748).

16

Mt Asaka: Like all place-names, apart from post-towns, Bashō has some allusion to poetry in mind, as well as often an interest in the original sense of the name.

katsumi (*Zizania latifolia*): In Bashō's day, there were two plants by this name: water-oat and iris. The former is more likely here. *Hana* means "flower," so the same plant in blossom. *Katsumi* is used in thatching especially for Boys' Day, May 5th, which in the old calendar was the beginning of midsummer.

Kurozuka cavern: Literally, Black Cave, legendary home of a demon in the guise of an old woman. Cf. Nōh play of the same name.

17

Shinobu-moji-zuri (*Davallia bullata*): A local grass used for rubbing dye into cloth placed on a famous granitic rock, and a regionally favorite way of creating a fresh and natural design. Word *shinobu*, as a verb, means "recalling times past," and it was believed that this particular rock when rubbed with young plants would reveal the image of one's beloved.

18

Satō Shōji: Satō Motoharu. *Shōji*: Title of a manor official (secretary-in-chief). His two sons, Tsugunobu and Tadanobu, lost their lives in defending that of their lord Yoshitsune. Their wives, to comfort their mother-in-law, put on the men's warrior gear as if in triumphal return.

The story finds reference in the Nōh drama, *Settai*.

the story of their heroism: Cf. Johnson again in his travels with Boswell (which have many interesting overlays with Bashō's journal; the differences also tell much): "To abstract the mind from all local emotion would be impossible, if it were endeavoured, and would be foolish, if it were possible. Whatever withdraws us from the power of our senses; whatever makes the past, the distant, or the future predominate over the present, advances us in the dignity of thinking beings. Far from me and from my friends, be such frigid philosophy as may conduct us indifferent and unmoved over any ground which has been dignified by wisdom, bravery, or virtue. That man is little to be envied whose patriotism would not gain force upon the plain of *Marathon* or whose piety would not grow warmer among the ruins of *Iona*!"

Weeping Rock: Located at Mt. Ken in China, named by poet Tu Yu, for a famous tomb there which, merely to look upon, it was said, caused one to weep.

Minamoto Yoshitsune (1159-1189): Perhaps the most celebrated of Japanese warriors, he was of the Genji clan. The stories, which are legion, may be found in the *Heike Monogatari* especially and in various Nōh and Kabuki plays (cf. A & G Halford, *The Kabuki Handbook*, pp 418-25 for summary).

Benkei: Priest of the Kamakura period, famous as one of Yoshitsune's cleverest and most devoted followers. Appears in various Nōh and Kabuki pieces. (v. Halford, *op. cit.*)

oi: Wickerwork chest for Buddhist gear.

paper standards: Alludes to paper carp, etc., seen flying above houses in Japan where families have sons for the May 5th festivity, although they are generally put out several weeks in advance.

Satsuki: Old calendar May; rice-planting month.

19

the usual trouble: diagnosed as diarrhea, though other guesses have been made.

fleas mosquitoes...: cf. *Chuang-tzu*: Bk. 14 with its counsel in the face of such: "See that naturalness is not lost, move with the wind."

20

Abumizuri: This is a good example of how Bashō uses place-names. Literally "stirrup-rubbing," it was evidently a narrow pass and evokes a "strait is the gate" feeling.

district of Kasashima: An example of Bashō's probably deliberate errors. The district was, in fact, that of Natori, but in terms of feeling, sound and overall structure, Bashō is right.

Tō-no-chūjō Sanekata (d. 998?): Tō refers to the Fujiwara clan. Famous as a poet and the lover of Sei Shōnagon of *Pillow Book* fame (cf. Waley). Exiled for insulting celebrated court calligrapher, Fujiwara-no-Yukinari. Known in exile as Lord of Mutsu. (In Oku.)

susuki grass of memory: Sedge planted at Sanekata's grave and mentioned in poem by Saigyō.

Minowa: Straw raincoat.

Kasashima: "Umbrella Isle."

21

Nōin-Hōshi (988–1050): Priest, then poet, of the Heian period. Influenced recluse literature, later established by Saigyō. Considered one of the thirty-six great poets of his period.

Kyohaku (?–1696): Disciple. Some selected poems in the *Minashiguri* (Hollow Chestnut) anthology.

22

Day of plaiting eaves: Formerly done on Boys' Day.

blue flags (Japanese *ayamegusa*): Plants of the iris family, evidently auspicious and indicative of strength and virility. Actually more nearly magenta in color.

hagi: Bush clover, having tiny pink or white blossoms.

Tsutsuki-ga-oka: Azalea Hill.

asebi (Pieris japonica): A member of the azalea family, having small white, bell-shaped clusters.

Konoshia: "Under Woods."

All place-names from poetry.

"Attendants, an umbrella...": Quoted from the *Kokinshū*, afamous anthology of Heian period. Cf. Keene, *Anthology of Japanese Lit.*

Yakushidō: Afamous shrine built by the feudal lord of Sendai, Date

Masamune (1565–1636).

Tenjin Shrine: Dedicated to priest and scholar Sugiwara Michizane (845–903) and built in 974. He was exiled in life and deified as Tenjin, with a temple in most Japanese towns. (Cf. Eliot, *op. cit.*, p. 183n.)

ah...: Cf. Pound's "Canto IV": "Saffron sandal so petals the narrow foot," (based on Catullus LXI: "*huc veni nives gerens/luteum pede soccum.*"

23

kokushu: Prefectural governor.

Tsubo-no-ishibumi: Oldest extant monument in Japan, erected in 712.

crosspoints: Northeast, northwest, southwest, southeast.

first year of Jinki: 724.

sixth year of Tempyō-hōji: 762.

Ono-no-ason Azumabito (d. 742): Military leader under three Emperors. Vanquished Ezo people and built Taga Castle. Titles italicized mean inspector and governer-general.

sangi and setsudoshi: Councillor (cabinet member) and commander of the defense of the Tōkai.

Tōkai: Eastern Sea (fifteen provinces of Tōkaido).

Tōzan: Eastern Mountain Region (thirteen provinces of Tōzando).

Time of Emperor Shōmu: 701–56.

24

Oki-no-ishi: A rock, in water, celebrated in poetry.

Sue-no-Matsuyama: "Pine Mountain Point," pine-clad slope near the sea; in fact, the sea, when seen from above, seems to flow around its base. Famous love poems refer to it. The section is full of images of fidelity.

"*wing and wing, branch and branch...*": Derived from Chinese poetry: Po Chü-i (772–843), as picked up via *Genji Monogatari*.

samidare: May rains.

"*Fishing boats....*:" From an anonymous poem in the *Kokinshū* mentioning Shiogama (literally, "salt pot").

Oku-jōruri: Dramatic back-country balladry, accompanied by *biwa (Japaanese lute)* or *shamisen* (Japanese mandolin), telling of Yoshitsune's coming to the Eastern provinces.

mai or *Kōwaka-mai*: A sort of simplified Nōh dance, originating in the Ashikaga period (after Kamakura), but in Bashō's day much on the wane.

25

kokushu: In this case, Date Masamune.

Izumi Saburō: Of the Fujiwara, he was the third son of Hidehira and the brother of Yasuhira, who was responsible for Yoshitsune's death. Killed at age twenty-three by his brother also, for being loyal to the famed leader.

Third Year of the Bunji: 1187.

26

"mulberry land": Chinese poeticism for Japan.

Dōtei: Lake Tung-t'ing in Hunan province (China). *Seiko:* Hsi-hu (*hu:* large lake, in Chinese) in the city of Hangchow. Literally, "West Lake." A famed spot, there is a famous painting by Mu Ch'i of *Dōtei* in autumn ,and Okakura in his *Book of Tea*, p. 98, writes of "...Linwosing, losing himself amid mysterious fragrance as he wandered in the twilight among the plum blossoms of the Western Lake." These are among the favorite images of Chinese landscape in Japanese eyes.

The description of Matsushima suggests the array of rocks and/or shrubs in Zen gardens.

Sekkō: Che-chiang: i.e., the Ch'ien-t'ang River in Chekiang Province, China, famous for its tidal bore.

Ōyamazumi: Mountain god of legend.

27

zazen: Religious meditation.

Ungozenji: Under the patronage of Date Tadamume (son of Masamune), he restored the Zuiganji temple. A monk of famous probity and religious influence (1583-1659).

crane: Image of longevity and good omen.

Sodō (1642-1716): Studied *haikai* with Kigin (1624-1705), Bashō's teacher, in Kyoto, but finally settled in Edo and became friendly with Bashō.

Hara Anteki: An Edo doctor, he wasd well-versed in *waka*.

Dakushi: Pen-name of warrior who, while on duty in Edo, got to know Bashō.

28

Zuiganji: Tendai temple originally in Hōjō (1205-1333) period, re-established as Rinzai.

Makabe-no-Heishirō (?-1273): Said to have visited China to study Ch'an Buddhism for nine years, he lived in Matsushima thereafter.

priesthood: To become a bonze.

Tō: T'ang country, or China.

tiles newly refurbished, walls gilded: This was done in 1610.

Kenbutsu Hijiri: Famed Buddhist priest of 12th century, he died aged eighty-two. He lived on Ojima. *Hijiri*: saint or sage or mahatma. Saigyō met him once at the sage's cave in Noto and later, much impressed, visited him at Matsushima.

29

pine of Aneha: Continually replanted. First celebrated in the Ise Monogatari (cf. Keene, *op. cit.*), where the pine is regarded as a woman.

Odae Bridge: From a love poem in the *Goshūishū* (1086) and *Genji Monogatari. Odae* literally means "breaking off life."

"where gold blossoms": Gold was first found in 749 in Oku. Quoted, from a poem by Otomo-no-Yakamochi for the Emperor, in the *Manyōshū* (vol. 18, no. 4097).

Sode: Literally, "sleeve." He has a tearful allusion from *Shin Gōshūishū* in mind.

Obuchi: Alludes to a plaintive love-poem in the *Gosenshū* (951).

Mano: Alludes to poem no. 396 in the *Manyōshū*, where a sense of distance is emphasized.

30

three generations: Refers to the Fujiwara clan (1094-1189); not associated with the famous Heian family. Hidehira was the last of the three generations. Said to be of Ainu descent, Hidehira's son, Yasuhira, was defeated by Minamoto-no-Yoritomo, the *shōgun* at Kamakura, though the former, at Yoritomo's conspiratorial instance, had killed Yoshitsune, Yoritomo's refugee brother.

"...as in a sleep": Alluding to the Nōh play *Kantan*, with its refrence to the dreamed-of-imperial-career of the Chinese scholar, Lu-sheng.

Kinkei: "Golden Birds," cock and hen.

Takadachi: Hill or high place.

Ezo: Ainu.

"*The county devastated...*": Adapted from a famous poem by Tu Fu.

Kanefusa: He was sixty-three when he died, loyally, with his lord Yoshitsune, when the castle at Takadachi was taken.

kyōdō: Sutra library.

images: Wooden statues.

Three Generals: The statues are, in fact, of Buddhist deities, but not unusually configuring particular people; here: Kiyohira, Motohira, and Hidehira, whose mummified remains rest in the coffins.

hikaridō: Literally, "Hall of Splendor," built in 1124.

three images of Buddha: Amida-Nyorai, Kannon and Seishi Bosatsu. A.N.: Shaka, world-teacher; Amida, savior. Kannon: figure of Mercy or Compassion; Seishi: Mahâsthâmaprâpta, in Chinese Ta-Shi-Chih. Cf. Eliot, *op. cit.*, pp. 128-9.)

The Seven Gems: Treasures, usually given as gold, silver, crystal, white and red corals, and emerald (cf. *Sutra of Everlasting Life*).

31

Ogurozaki: Allusion to poem in the *Kokinshū*, including reference to Mitsu-no-kojima: "Three Isles," suggesting Bashō thinks of friends left behind.

suspiciously: Cf. *Chuang-tzu*, Bk. 13, v. 60.

fleas lice: Cf. Martin Buber on *The Teaching of the Tao*: "Lao-tzu says to Khung-tsu: 'as horseflies keep one awake the whole night, so this talk of love of mankind and righteousness plagues me. Strive to bring the world back to its original simplicity,'" which can also refer to No. 19.

32

beyond bird cry: Suggested by poems of Tu Fu and Wang An-shih (1021–86).

shino: Small bamboo.

33

Seifū (1651–1721): Studied *haikai* in Kyoto with Teitoku school, but pupil at this point and admirer of Bashō. Wealthy cosmetic (*beni*-dye) merchant. The safflower (*beni*), used in Japanese cosmetics, grew in abundance near Obanazawa.

worm room: Of course, the silkworm; the "croaker" is the humble demon, the frog.

antique: Women working at silkworm care evidently behaved and dressed (quite plainly) in a fashion reminiscent of a simpler, more antique time. Readers often fail to note Bashō's unfailing interest in the female element; it is a grace-note throughout and gives richness to the whole.

34

Jikaku Daishi (Ennin, during his lifetime, 794–864): Tendai leader of his day, who had studied Buddhism nine years in China (from 838), sympathetic to Shingon and Amidism (cf. Eliot, *op. cit.*).

35

seeds of old haikai: Refers to the Teimon (Teitoku) school or Danrin (Sōin) school, Bashō's own "new" superseded all.

collection: aArenka, composed at a party there.

reed-flute...: Alluding to Mongols in Chinese poetry, whose plaintive instruments made distant listeners feel how far from home they were.

Goten: Scattered go (chess) stones.

Hayabusa: Literally, swooping falcon

inabune: Literally rice-boat," in which sheaves of feudal tithings were carried, but also refers to the negative of antique times implied in the pun of "ina-"; a poem in the *Kokinshū* connects it also with the Mogamigawa, a love-poem, but its hesitant negative here suggests Bashō's apprehension shooting the rapids.

Shiraito: "White Thread."

Sennindō: Literally, hermit's hall, alluding to Yoshitsune's retainer, Hitachibō Kaison's, dwelling, now a shrine, where he retired as a mountain hermit after the battle with the Heike. A figure of longevity, Bashō's mention of it is almost a prayer.

36

Zushi Sakichi (pen-name: Rogan): Poet and dyeing-merchant for *yamabushi* clothing.

bettō-dai: Deputy intendant at temple.

Ajari (Skt. âcârya): Teacher (cf. rabbi) or master, a priestly degree in Tendai and Shingon sects.

Perfuming snow: Suggests a passage in the Confucian *Li Chi* (Book of Rites): "The perfumed wind comes from the South." It implies a warm and gracious atmosphere, as well as refreshing clarity.

Minamidami: South Valley.

Gongen: Avatar of Buddha in Ryōbu Shinto.

Nōjo Daishi: Should be Taishi, third prince of Emperor Sushun (588–92).

Engishiki: Fifty-volume compilation of local rites and customs completed under the Emperor Daigo, 927.

Dewa: Literally, feather-bearing.

Fudoki: Records of the Natural Features of the various imperial provinces, prepared at the instance of the Empress Gemmyō in 712. Some are still extant.

Bukō: Edo area.

shi-kan: Chinese: Chih-kuan; Sanskrit: Samatha and Vipassanâ, i.e., calm and insight, the central doctrine of the Tendai sect (cf. Eliot, *op. cit.*, pp. 334–5). Based on a work by Chih I (538–597), written in 594, Chinese founder of the T'ien-t'ai sect. Essentially Indian thought. A quote by Eliot, who admits his inability to grasp it, may illuminate the doctrine a little: (from Chih I) "A bright mirror take as illustration. Brightness is *k'ung*; image *chia*; the mirror *chung*. Not joined, not divided: combined and separate just as they are."

The "trinity" (or "triad") of temples suggests the "three truths" of the Tendai sect: *Isshin Sangan*, as exemplified above and requiring preparation, training and concentration.

endonyuz ū: Tendai doctrine implying sudden and utter enlightenment, the light one carries and the light of the moon suddenly merging in a complete sphere.

37

Gassan: lit. "Moon Mountain." Highest of the mountains of traditional sanctity given here.

Yūshime: Paper garland often worn by mountain priests.

hōkan: Cotton headgear with pointed ends.

gōriki: Literally, strong power, a mountain guide, probably *uamabushi*.

Ryūsen: Literally Dragon Spring, reputed to have existed in South China.

Kanshō and Bakuya: Kan-chiang and *Mo-yeh* in Chinese, are two swords— Bashō doesn't mention the third, *Lung-yüan*—famed in Chinese legend.

The first is male, the second, female. (AF) cf. *Chuang-tzu*, Book 23, sect 8 (Legge), fn 2. Cf. the Nōh play *Kokaji*.

slow blossoms: Cf. the tea-master Rikyū's poem, often quoted for its "wabi" quality (in the *Book of Tea*): "For those desiring flowers/Let me show/The full-blown spring/That dwells within/The struggling buds of/Snow-clad hills."

"plum...blazing...": Suggestive of *satori*. Allusion to a poem by Wang Wei (701–61), famed Chinese poet.

Gyōson Sōjō (?–1135): Buddhist priest-poet of the Minamoto family. Poem referred to speaks of the isolation of mountain cherry blossoms. From the *Kinyōshū* (1125).

the code: Unwritten rule not to write or speak of what goes on or is seen on religious premises.

·san: Mountain, i.e., temple.

"at Yudono...": Mountain's name literally means "bath room," and "wetting one's sleeve" is the indirect phrase for tears. One feels the exceeding release of feeling here, a cleansing.

penny stepping-stones: Sora refers to the custom there of not picking up the good luck largesse bestowed by pilgrims at the mountain site. They evidently form a trail to the temple. Sora's poem sounds almost humorous after Bashō's—but no less devout for that.

38

round: Renka

Nagayama Shigeyuki: His pen-name was Jūkō. A samurai poet, he met Bashō in Edo and became a disciple.

En-an Fugyoku (?–1697): A disciple evidently, but this is the clearest reference to him there is.

Atsumi: "Hot Sea."'

Fuku-ura: "Windy Harbor."

39

heart's inch-space: Chinese phrase. Cf. Lu Chi's *Wen Fu* (*New Mexico Quarterly*, Autumn 1952): "We lock infinity into a square foot of silk; pour a deluge from the inch-space of the heart." Cf. n. 3. (pp. 173–4) of Coomaraswamy's *The Transformation of Nature in Art*: "immanent space of the heart"; *antarhrdaya-ākāsa*: space in the heart; i.e., innermost core of being.

Jingū Kōgū: Empress, d. 269.

hōjō: Ten foot square chamber (front room) in Zen temple.

Shiogoshi: Tidal flooding.

Seishi: In Chinese: *Hsi-shih,* a famous Chinese beauty of antiquity. Referred
to in the poem "maybe rain an enchantment..." by Su Tung-p'o (Su
Shih, 1036–1101). Bashō quotes it above. Cf. Blyth, *Haiku,* Vol. 3, page
303.

silk-tree blossoms: A tree of the mimosa family, but the Japanese word "nemu-
no-hana" has a play on the verb *nemu,* "to sleep." In fact, the leaves fold
shut at night. It has a pale orange blossom.

what's to eat...: Sora refers to the local festival of its tutelary god Myōjin,
where no meat or fish are eaten. The festival normally falls on the
eighth day of the eighth lunar month.

panels: The fishermen would remove the doors of their huts in summer,
which, like all such elements in Japanese houses, are grooved rather
than hinged and easily removable, and picnic on them.

vow vowed: Ezra Pound's "fish-hawk" in Ode no. 1 in *The Classic Anthology.*
(Cf. Legge, *Chinese Classics,* Vol. 4, p. 3, fn. to Ode no. 1) (AF). The
bird, as Sora states, nests on rocks close to the tide and remains faith-
ful to his brood even in the teeth of it.

40

Nezu: "Mouse."

poetry's month...: July, in the old calendar. Written on the eve of the
Tanabata Festival, which celebrates the annual proximity of two stars
identified in ancient myths as a man and wife who angered God, who
thus banished the husband to the Milky Way. Poems would be written
about stars and hung in trees. It is still celebrated in Japan.

wild seas: Cf. Tu Fu (*Poems of the Late T'ang,* Graham, Penguin, p. 46):
"After sudden rain, a clear autumn night./On golden waves the sparkle
of the Jewelled Cord./The River of Heaven white from eternity...."

Sado: Famed island off the west coast of Honshū where many political
exiles were sent; *the great star stream,* literally "Heaven's river," is our
Milky Way.

41

Place-names of sentiment: *Oyashirazu*: literally, parent lost; *Koshirazu*: child lost; *Inumodori*: dog turning back; *Komagaeshi*: horse turned back. Singular may be plural in Japanese; only eyes can tell.

Hokkoku: North Country.

play-girls: Literal, though often translated as prostitutes, which is misleading in many ways

"*On the strand...*": from the *Shinkokinshū*. Cf. Ortega y Gasset's description of the female element in Cervantes' *Exemplary Tales*: "worn-out, wandering young ladies who sigh deeply in the rooms of inns and speak of their maltreated virginity in Ciceronian style."

By the grace of your robes: Bashō and Sora are evidently mistaken for monks, but Bashō's haiku becomes a prayer in their behalf, as well as a recognition of joined world. Note how Bashō rings changes on the word "*hagi*" throughout the journal. (Also the most commonly mentioned flower, t in the *Manyōshū*, occurring, it is said, no less than 138 times!) The shrines at Ise, it might be noted, were a famous excuse for young lovers to escape their families and find rendezvous.

in the one house: This poem, with its brief note by Bashō—"Sora hearing this wrote it down"—has implications. Apparently Bashō was shy of keeping it himself. It also corroborates two facts: 1) that Bashō composed his poems aloud often, or simply in his head and 2) that the journal was edited and prepared afterwards. That Bashō reconsidered and put the poem in bespeaks particular affection for it, extending it beyond any mere vulgarity.

hagi: Usually translated as "bush-clover," recently introduced for improved ecology into U.S. agriculture.

42

waves of wisteria: Alluding to poem in the *Manyōshū* about Tako.

43

the art: That of haikai.

44

Komatsu: "Small Pine" or "Young Pine."

Sanemori: His story is told in *Heike Monogatari*, made into a Nōh play of the same name by Zeami. The word "cruel" in the *haiku* is drawn from the Nōh. The oldest warrior killed fighting for the Taira clan against the Genji (Minamoto), he had dyed his hair black so as not to be spared. Originally, as a young man, had fought for the Genji.

nishiki: Imperial brocade.

45

Kannondō: Temple to goddess (god) of mercy.

Daiji Haihi: Goddess (God) of Great Mercy. Emperor Kazan named the place Nata in 986.

kaya: Zebra grass.

Ishiyama: Bashō lived for some time in the Genjūan on Ishiyama (Stone Mountain) in Omi province (cf. *Haikai and Haiku*, p. xiii.).

no whiter: White often means transparent in Japanese and is the color of autumn. Spring is blue, summer red, and winter black.

46

Ariake: Evidently Bashō erred, consciously or unconsciously, and intended reference to Arima, nine miles from Kobe, upland, famed for its mineral springs. (Cf. opening of the Noh play *Tadanori* for ancient reference.)

kiku: Our unwieldly word chrysanthemum.

leave kiku unplucked: Cf. *Kiku Jidō* (sometimes known as *Makura Jidō*), Nōh play. The recipe for longevity is given here. The spa water is odorous as well as bracing. Bashō doesn't hide his aches, though he won't exaggerate them either, and his satisfactions also find full breath.

Teishitsu: Died in 1675.

Raku: Old word for Kyoto, or a section of it.

Teitoku (1571–1653): Kyoto-born head of Teimon school and the literary scholar who tried to "classicize *haikai* and return to *renga*" (cf. *Haikai and Haiku*, NGS, p.x.).

judge: I.e., of a haikai contest.

like the parting of a pair of wild geese: There is a double allusion here, one from Chinese poetry and the other very personal. Bashō had written a very early *haiku* on the deeply-moving occasion of his young lord Sengin's death (Bashō was possibly still in his teens): "Parting from his friends/A wild goose goes its way/Soon to be beyond the clouds." (clumsy version found in *Haikai and Haiku*, p. 142).

efface the inscription: On the hinoki-strip hat (*kasa*) pilgrims always had a blessing inscribed: "Between heaven and earth Buddha and I share the journey."

47

ink-slab: Shallow ink dish, usually of stone.

sweeping the yard: Bashō's hasty exit, with appointments in mind, evokes this poem of apology for abruptness. Generally a guest of such a temple would sweep the yard a little in compensation for accommodations. Bashō's sensibility (*fūryū*) indicated by his feeling the "rightness" of the fallen leaves.

48

Throughout the long night...: Poem attributed to Saigyō; also quoted near the start of the Noh *Yamauba*.

one finger too many: Suggests *Chuang-tzu*, Bk. VIII, 3. "Webbed toes adding useless flesh to feet, extra fingers planted useless flesh to hands, so overindulgence, etc."

49

Hokushi (166-1718): Sword-sharpener by trade, became disciple of Bashōon this trip.

fan wrenched apart...: The ubiquitous fan would be customarily destroyed at summer's end.

fifty chō: About 3.2 miles.

a thousand li from Hōki: From Chinese *Book of Odes*. Hōki, the imperial seat, here implies Kyoto.

Dōgenzenji (1200-53): Brought Sōtō (Ts'ao-T'ung) Zen into Japan (1253). Studied Zen under Eisai (founder of the Rinzai sect). Went to China in 1223. Built Eiheiji, which Eliot (*op. cit.*, p. 284) calls "the finest monastery in Japan."

50

Yūgao and hechima: Kinds of gourds.

keitō: Cock's comb.

hahakigi: Broom cypress.

gobō: Buddhist priest, bonze.

kimono: Simply, clothing, but Japanese style.

guidepost: Quite accurate. Actually a branch torn off and stuck in the ground to indicate directions along by-ways.

51

Kaeru: "Return."

Emperor Chūai: Ruled approximately 192-200.

Yugyō Shōnin (Ippen, 1239-1289): Originally a Tendai priest, he made much of the Nembutsu (repeated utterance of Buddha's name). A curious dance is also part of his evangelical sect. Popularly known by the name given here, which means "wandering priest." Cf. the Nōh *Yugyō Yanagi*.

Yugyō: Means sand-carrying.

52

small shells: The *masuo (Sanguinolaria elongata Lamarock)*, suggesting a poem by Saigyō.

warigo: Divided lunch box.

sasae: Bamboo bottle for *sake*.

Hokke: Buddhist sect.

Suma: Cf. book of that name in the Cenji Monogatari.

53

Rotsū (1651 ?-1739?): Met Bashō in Edo in 1688. He had a difficult personality and became estranged from Bashō in 1692, but Bashō remained concerned about him.

Etsujin (1656?-1739): An early disciple and an obstinate and irascible man, he debated Shikō literary matters after Bashō's death in a series of tracts.

Jokō (?-1706): Former samurai. Priest and disciple.

Zensenshi: From Ogaki, no more known.

Keikō father and sons: Father (1673-1735); all three sons were Bashō's disciples.

Nagatsuki: Literally, "long month, or moon."

ceremonial moving at Ise: The sacred Shinto shrines—especially the shrine of the Sun goddess, Ama-terasu, regarded as the founder of Japan—and a kind of Japanese Mecca. The shrines are rebuilt every twenty years (or in the 21st year), September 10–13 by the old calendar. Bashō may also here have in mind a *waka* by Saigyō (quoted by Blyth, *op. cit.*, Vol. 2, p. 138), which is a poem of deep gratitude.

back in the boat again: Referring us to the start of the journal, of the journey.

hamaguri: Large native clam

clam/shell and innards parting . . . : A most difficult poem to bring across because it's full of inner wordplay. The *romaji* goes: *hamaguri-no/fatami-ni wakare/yubu aki-zo.* *Futami*, the key-word, is the place-name of a bay famous for its clams where sunrise may be seen between rocks. *Futa* means "lids" and *mi* both "innards" and "to see." The shell has opened; Bashō is on the move again. "Departing fall" sounds "departing spring" and the breath resumes at a deeper fuller pitch.

EPILOGUE

Most texts of the *Oku-no-hosomichi* close with the famed calligrapher Soryū's "Epilogue." It was he, at Bashō's call, who, in 1694, copied out the version from which we and all readers today draw sustenance. Kojin refers to the weaver-demon of China, whose tears turn into jewels.

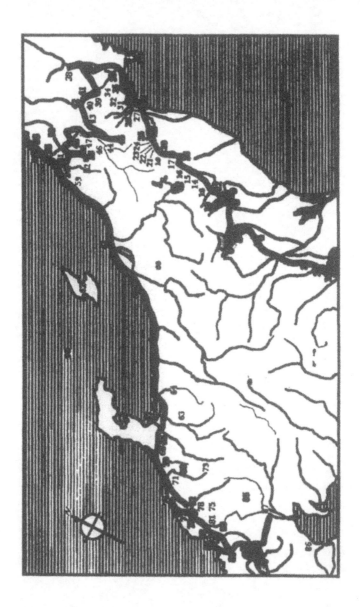

THE FAR TOWNS

1. Edo (Tokyo)
2. Senju
3. Sōka
4. Muro-no-Yashima
5. Imaichi
6. Nikkō
7. Mt. Kurokami
8. Kurobane
9. Unganji
10. Sesshōseki
11. Ashino
12. Shirakawa Barrier
13. Shirakawa
14. Kagenuma
15. Sukagawa
16. Hihada
17. Nihonmatsu
18. Kurozuka
19. Fukushima
20. Shinobu
21. Se-no-ue
22. Iizuka
23. Ko-ori
24. Okido
25. Abumizuri
26. Shiroishi
27. Takekuma's Pine
28. Iwanuma
29. Kasashima
30. Natorigawa R.
31. Sendai
32. Taga Castle
33. Sue-no-Matsuyama
34. Shiogama
35. Matsushima
36. Ishi-no-maki
37. Mt. Kinka
38. Hiraizumi
39. Iwade
40. Ogurozaki
41. Narugo
42. Shitomae
43. Obanazawa
44. Yamagata
45. Ryūshakuji
46. Mogamigawa R.
47. Oishida
48. Shiraito Falls

COMPANIONS FOR THE JOURNEY SERIES

This series presents inspirational work by well-known writers
in a small-book format designed to be carried along
on your journey through life.

Volume 6
A Zen Forest: Zen Sayings
Translated by Soiku Shigematsu
Preface by Gary Snyder
1-893996-30-1   5 x 7   140 pages $14.00

Volume 5
Back Roads to Far Towns
Basho's Travel Journal
Translated by Cid Corman
1-893996-31-X   5 x 7   128 pages $13.00

Volume 4
Heaven My Blanket, Earth My Pillow
Poems from Sung Dynasty China by Yang Wan-Li
Translated by Jonathan Chaves
1-893996-29-8   5 x 7   120 pages $14.00

Volume 3
10,000 Dawns
The Love Poems of Yvan and Claire and Goll
Translated by Thomas Rain Crowe and Nan Watkins
1-893996-27-1   5 x 7   96 pages $13.00

Volume 2
There Is No Road
Proverbs by Antonio Machado
Translated by Mary G. Berg & Dennis Maloney
1-893996-66-2   5 x 7   120 pages $14.00

Volume 1
Wild Ways: Zen Poems of Ikkyu
Translated by John Stevens
1-893996-65-4   5 x 7   128 pages $14.00